A **TRUE** BOOK™

My United States

Massachusetts

CODY CRANE

Children's Press®
An Imprint of Scholastic Inc.

Content Consultant

James Wolfinger, PhD, Associate Dean and Professor
College of Education, DePaul University, Chicago, Illinois

Library of Congress Cataloging-in-Publication Data
Names: Crane, Cody, author.
Title: Massachusetts / by Cody Crane.
Description: New York, NY : Children's Press, an imprint of Scholastic Inc., 2018. | Series: A true book | Includes bibliographical
    references and index.
Identifiers: LCCN 2017002075| ISBN 9780531252598 (library binding) | ISBN 9780531232897 (pbk.)
Subjects: LCSH: Massachusetts—Juvenile literature.
Classification: LCC E404 .C926 2018 | DDC 974.4—dc23
LC record available at https://lccn.loc.gov/2017002075

Photos ©: cover: Amanda Hall/robertharding/Getty Images; back cover bottom: Sonar Technician (Submarine) 2nd Class
Thomas Rooney/U.S. Navy; back cover ribbon: AliceLiddelle/Getty Images; 3 bottom: Joseph Sohm/Shutterstock; 3 map: Jim
McMahon; 4 right: Flowerphotos/Eye Ubiquitous/Superstock, Inc.; 4 left: Richard Robinson/Minden Pictures; 5 bottom: Dora
Zett/Shutterstock; 5 top: Boston Globe/Getty Images; 7 center bottom: Steve Vidler/Superstock, Inc.; 7 center top: Marcio Jose
Bastos Silva/Shutterstock; 7 top: RosaIreneBetancourt 12/Alamy Images; 7 bottom: Richard Robinson/Minden Pictures; 8-9:
Sean Pavone/Shutterstock; 11 background: Visions of America/Superstock, Inc.; 11 man: Boston Globe/Getty Images; 12: Steve
Dunwell/Getty Images; 13: Bloomberg/Getty Images; 14: MyLoupe/Getty Images; 15: Jeffrey Rotman/Alamy Images; 16-17:
Hemis/Alamy Images; 19: Everett - Art/Shutterstock; 20: Tigatelu/Dreamstime; 22 right: Pakmor/Shutterstock; 22 left: Atlaspix/
Shutterstock; 23 center right: Rex May/Alamy Images; 23 bottom left: Flowerphotos/Eye Ubiquitous/Superstock, Inc.; 23 bottom
right: Lightspring/Shutterstock; 23 top right: istetiana/Shutterstock; 23 top left: Alan Murphy/BIA/Minden Pictures /Superstock,
Inc.; 23 center left: Dora Zett/Shutterstock; 24-25: DEA Picture Library/Getty Images; 27: North Wind Picture Archives/Alamy
Images; 29: Superstock, Inc.; 30: Niday Picture Library/Alamy Images; 31: GraphicaArtis/Getty Images; 32 left: MPI/Getty Images;
32 right: Steve Dunwell/Getty Images; 33 right: Atlaspix/Shutterstock; 33 center: Niday Picture Library/Alamy Images; 33 left:
Superstock, Inc.; 34-35: Boston Globe/Getty Images; 36: Boston Globe/Getty Images; 37: Boston Globe/Getty Images; 38:
Boston Globe/Getty Images; 39: mizoula/iStockphoto; 40 bottom: Alexandra Grablewski/Exactostock-1527/Superstock, Inc.; 40
background: PepitoPhotos/iStockphoto; 41: Melvyn Longhurst/Alamy Images; 42 top left: FineArt/Alamy Images; 42 top right:
Science History Images/Alamy Images; 42 bottom left: RGB Ventures/SuperStock/Alamy Images; 42 bottom right: Niday Picture
Library/Alamy Images; 43 top left: World History Archive/Alamy Images; 43 top right: Mary Evans Picture Library/Alamy Images;
43 center: FPG/Getty Images; 43 bottom left: Granamour Weems Collection/Alamy Images; 43 bottom center: John Bryson/Getty
Images; 43 bottom right: NASA/Superstock, Inc.; 44 bottom right: f11photo/Shutterstock; 44 top: Ken Wolter/Shutterstock; 44
center: martellostudio/Shutterstock; 44 bottom left: Molly Lynch/AA World Travel/Topfoto/The Image Works; 45 top: Songquan
Deng/Shutterstock; 45 center: Jeff Rotman/Getty Images; 45 bottom: Flowerphotos/Eye Ubiquitous/Superstock, Inc.

Maps by Map Hero, Inc.

Front cover: A swan boat in Boston

**Back cover: The USS *Constitution*
in Boston Harbor**

Welcome to Massachusetts

UNITED STATES

Massachusetts

Find the Truth!

Everything you are about to read is true *except* for one of the sentences on this page.

Which one is **TRUE**?

T or F Massachusetts is named after the ship its first settlers arrived on.

T or F Cranberries are one of Massachusetts's biggest crops.

Massachusetts
BLUEZ 3
The Spirit of America

Find the answers in this book.

3

Contents

THE BIG TRUTH!

Cranberries

What Represents Massachusetts?

Shark

Runners finish the Boston Marathon.

3 History

How did Massachusetts become
the state it is today?

4 Culture

What do the people of Massachusetts
do for work and fun?

Boston terrier

This Is Massachusetts!

MAINE

NEW YORK

VERMONT

NEW HAMPSHIRE

ATLANTIC OCEAN

Natural Bridge State Park

NORTH ADAMS

Berkshire Taconic Region

Mount Greylock

The Big Chair

Connecticut Valley

Walden Pond

LOWELL

GLOUCESTER

SALEM

Old North Church, Boston

PITTSFIELD

MASSACHUSETTS

LEOMINSTER

Connecticut

LEXINGTON

Concord and Lexington

2

BOSTON

3

Province

1

Tanglewood Music Center

WORCESTER

Harvard University

Charles

Boston Common

PLYMOUTH

SPRINGFIELD

VE RI TAS

HARVARD

CAPE COD BAY

Naismith Memorial Basketball Hall of Fame

RHODE ISLAND

CONNECTICUT

NEW BEDFORD

HYANNIS

Cape Co

4

Aquinnah Cliffs

New Bedford Whaling National Historic Park

Woods Hole Oceanographic Institution

Martha's Vineyard

Nantu Isla

NEW YORK

ATLANTIC OCEAN

0   20
Miles

N
W   E
S

① Tanglewood Music Center

Located in the Berkshire Hills, this outdoor venue is a great place to see a musical performance. It is the summer home of the Boston Symphony Orchestra.

② Harvard University

Harvard is the nation's oldest university—and one of its most respected. Visitors can stroll through campus or check out the Harvard Museum of Natural History.

③ Boston

One of the country's oldest cities, Boston is packed with fun things to do. It is also home to many important historical sites.

④ Woods Hole Oceanographic Institution

Located on Cape Cod, Woods Hole Oceanographic Institution is the largest marine research facility in the United States. Its scientists study the many animal species found in the nearby ocean waters.

Boston's subway system is known as the T.

CHAPTER 1

Land and Wildlife

What do basketball, baked beans, and chocolate chip cookies have in common? They were all invented in Massachusetts! This state is one of six that make up the New England region in the northeastern United States. Massachusetts is small, but it has helped shape the history and culture of America in a big way.

This map shows where the higher (yellow and orange) and lower (green) areas are in the state.

Mixed Landscape

Massachusetts has roughly 200 miles (322 kilometers) of coastline. That's not counting all of the state's tiny inlets and harbors. Measure those and the coastline grows to about 1,500 miles (2,414 km)! The low-lying area along the coast contains beaches, marshes, and **bogs**. Inland Massachusetts is made up of valleys and rolling hills. The highest terrain is found in western Massachusetts. This area is called the Berkshire Hills.

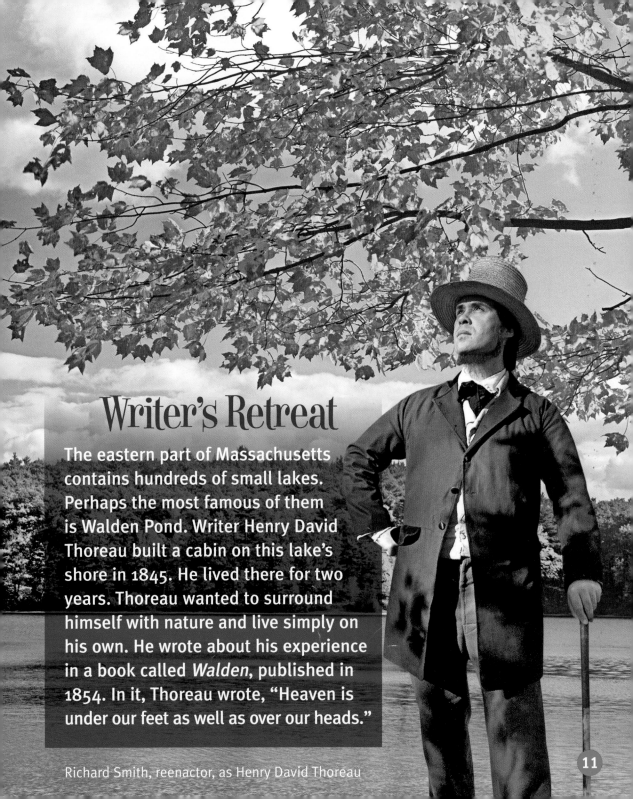

Writer's Retreat

The eastern part of Massachusetts contains hundreds of small lakes. Perhaps the most famous of them is Walden Pond. Writer Henry David Thoreau built a cabin on this lake's shore in 1845. He lived there for two years. Thoreau wanted to surround himself with nature and live simply on his own. He wrote about his experience in a book called *Walden*, published in 1854. In it, Thoreau wrote, "Heaven is under our feet as well as over our heads."

Richard Smith, reenactor, as Henry David Thoreau

Provincetown lies at the tip of a peninsula called Cape Cod.

From Lakes to Rivers

Along Massachusetts's coast lies Cape Cod. This **peninsula** looks like a big fishhook. It is named for the codfish that were once caught there in huge numbers. The cape's bogs are great for growing one of the state's biggest crops—cranberries.

The Quabbin Reservoir lies in central Massachusetts. Built to supply water to Boston, it is the state's largest lake. Nearby, the Connecticut River winds through a valley. People grow apples, vegetables, and Christmas trees in the area's rich soil.

Coastal Climate

Winters in western Massachusetts can be long, cold, and snowy. Winters are milder near the ocean, but summers there are hotter. The state's warmest month is July, with temperatures reaching above 80 degrees Fahrenheit (27 degrees Celsius). The coldest month is January, when temperatures dip well below freezing. During the winter, strong storms called northeasters can hit the state. Hurricanes are a threat in the summer and fall.

A single northeaster can dump 30 to 50 inches (76 to 127 centimeters) of snow on Massachusetts.

MAXIMUM TEMPERATURE	MINIMUM TEMPERATURE
107°F	-35°F

Mount Greylock in the Berkshire Hills is the highest point in Massachusetts.

Vast Woodlands

More than 60 percent of Massachusetts is covered in forests. People head to the Berkshires in the fall to see the trees' leaves change color. Pines and oaks grow near the coast. There are also marshes there that are filled with grasses. If you're lucky, you may spot a pink or white mayflower, the state flower. Sadly, this sweet-smelling plant is **endangered**. You will rarely see its pink or white blooms in the wild.

Wonderful Wildlife

A range of mammals fills the state's forests. Deer are the largest and most common. Hundreds of bird species visit Massachusetts or live there year-round. One permanent resident is the wild turkey, a popular hunting target and the state game, or hunted, bird. Sea life is a major part of the state's wildlife and of local culture. People fish in the ocean, rivers, and lakes for cod, haddock, shrimp, and oysters.

People have fished Massachusetts's coastal waters for centuries.

Massachusetts's constitution is the oldest still in use in the world.

Government

Boston has been a capital city since Massachusetts was founded as a colony in the early 1600s. Today, this historic city remains the center of activity for the state's elected leaders. They gather in the Massachusetts State House, which was completed in 1798, to make the state's laws.

The Three Branches

Massachusetts's state government is divided into three branches. The governor heads the executive branch, which manages the business of the state.

The legislative branch is called the General Court. Its Senate and House of Representatives make the state's laws.

The courts of the judicial branch hear cases and interpret the state's laws.

MASSACHUSETTS'S STATE GOVERNMENT

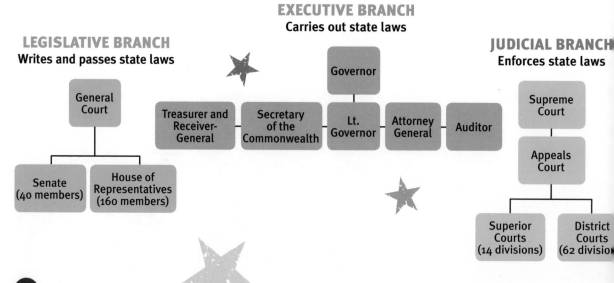

EXECUTIVE BRANCH
Carries out state laws

LEGISLATIVE BRANCH
Writes and passes state laws

JUDICIAL BRANCH
Enforces state laws

General Court

Treasurer and Receiver-General

Secretary of the Commonwealth

Governor

Lt. Governor

Attorney General

Auditor

Supreme Court

Appeals Court

Senate (40 members)

House of Representatives (160 members)

Superior Courts (14 divisions)

District Courts (62 division

John Adams was an important figure in Boston and across the country during and after the Revolutionary War.

The Massachusetts Constitution

Massachusetts adopted its constitution in 1780. The document was written by John Adams, an important figure in the American colonies' fight for independence who later became the country's second president. In the constitution, Adams called the state the "Commonwealth of Massachusetts." The word *commonwealth* means the state was founded for the good of its people.

In the National Government

Each state sends elected officials to represent it in the U.S. Congress. Like every state, Massachusetts has two senators. The U.S. House of Representatives relies on a state's population to determine its numbers. Massachusetts has nine representatives in the House.

Every four years, states vote on the next U.S. president. Each state has a number of electoral votes based on its number of members in Congress. Massachusetts has 11 electoral votes.

2 senators and 9 representatives

11 electoral votes

With 11 electoral votes, Massachusetts's voice in presidential elections is about average.

Representing Massachusetts

Elected officials in Massachusetts represent a population with a range of interests, lifestyles, and backgrounds.

Ethnicity (2015 estimates)

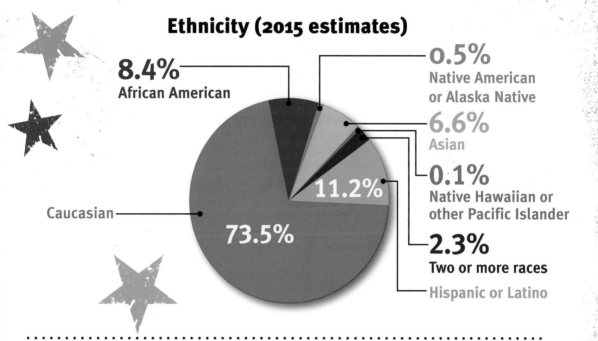

8.4%
African American

73.5%
Caucasian

11.2%

0.5%
Native American or Alaska Native

6.6%
Asian

0.1%
Native Hawaiian or other Pacific Islander

2.3%
Two or more races

Hispanic or Latino

41% of the population have a degree beyond high school.

62% own their own homes.

92% live in cities.

16% of Massachusetts residents were born in other countries.

90% of the population graduated from high school.

23% speak a language other than English at home.

What Represents Massachusetts?

States choose specific animals, plants, and objects to represent the values and characteristics of the land and its people. Find out why these symbols were chosen to represent Massachusetts or discover surprising curiosities about them.

Seal

Massachusetts's state seal bears the same image as its state flag. Around the design are the Latin words, *Sigillum Reipublicae Massachusettensis* ("Seal of the Republic of Massachusetts").

Flag

Massachusetts's flag depicts a Native American holding an arrow pointing down, representing peace. A star above his shoulder shows that Massachusetts was one of the original 13 colonies. The state's motto is shown in Latin. It means, "By the sword we seek peace, but peace only under liberty." The arm and sword above the shield represent this motto.

Boston Cream Pie

STATE DESSERT

This pie beat the chocolate chip cookie and Indian pudding to become the state dessert in 1996.

Black-Capped Chickadee

STATE BIRD

The chickadee is named for its "chick-a-dee-dee" call.

Mayflower

STATE FLOWER

Though the mayflower has been the state flower since 1918, it has been considered endangered since 1925.

Boston Terrier

STATE DOG

In 1869, this dog became the first purebred dog breed developed in the United States.

Cranberry

STATE BERRY

A grade school class worked two years to make the cranberry the official Massachusetts state berry.

Basketball

STATE SPORT

Dr. James Naismith invented basketball one summer day in 1891 in Springfield.

The English language contains many Algonquin words. They include Massachusetts, hickory, moose, squash, and woodchuck.

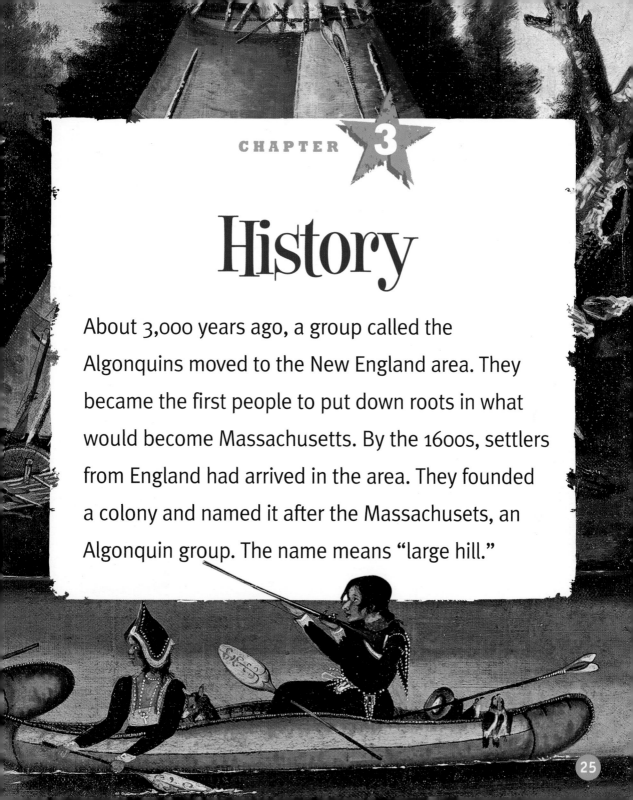

CHAPTER 3

History

About 3,000 years ago, a group called the Algonquins moved to the New England area. They became the first people to put down roots in what would become Massachusetts. By the 1600s, settlers from England had arrived in the area. They founded a colony and named it after the Massachusets, an Algonquin group. The name means "large hill."

First People

The Algonquins lived in villages made up of domed huts called wigwams. Men made the homes' frames from trees. Women wove mats to cover the walls and roofs of these frames. The Algonquins moved their camps to different spots to find food. They built canoes to sail off the coast and fish. They hunted deer, bears, moose, and smaller animals with bows and arrows. The Algonquins gathered wild berries, nuts, and shellfish. They also grew crops such as beans, corn, and squash.

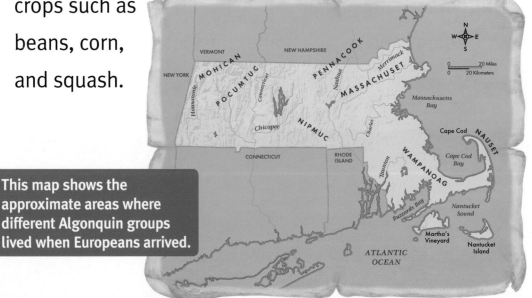

This map shows the approximate areas where different Algonquin groups lived when Europeans arrived.

Native Americans in Massachusetts mainly planted beans, corn, and squash. These crops were known as the Three Sisters.

Algonquin Life

Women and men had different roles in Algonquin culture. Women cared for children. They also tended crops, cooked, and made clothing. Men fished, hunted, and cleared land for farming. They built wigwams and canoes and protected their villages. Grandparents, parents, and children often lived together. Elders taught children about their culture's history. The Algonquins didn't have a written language, so families gathered to share stories about traditions, beliefs, and past events.

European Settlers

In 1602, explorer Bartholomew Gosnold sailed across the Atlantic Ocean from England to Massachusetts Bay. He named Cape Cod after the many codfish found there. Traders soon followed. On November 21, 1620, a ship called the *Mayflower* arrived in Massachusetts. Some passengers were escaping religious **persecution** in England. They formed a settlement called Plymouth. With little food, they barely survived the cold New England winter. They would not have made it without help from Native Americans.

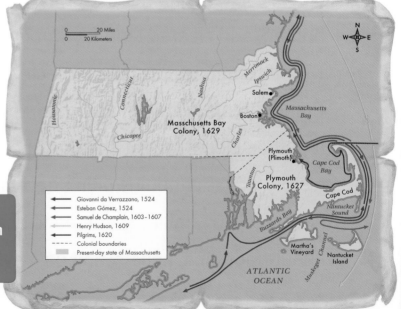

This map shows the routes explorers from Europe took around Massachusetts.

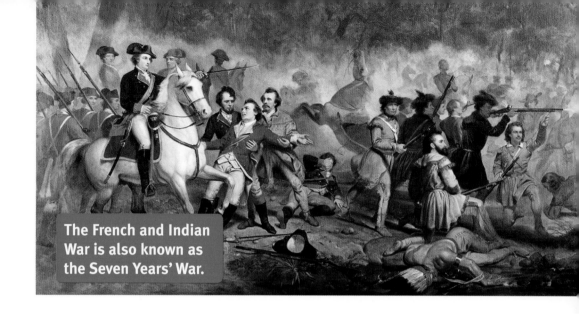

The French and Indian War is also known as the Seven Years' War.

Struggling Colony

In 1629, England created the Massachusetts Bay Colony. Boston became its capital. More colonists arrived and took over land that native people relied on for survival. This sparked fighting between the two groups. Then came the French and Indian War. From 1754 to 1763, Great Britain and its colonies fought against France and its Native American **allies**. The British won control of much of eastern North America. But the war was costly, so Great Britain taxed its colonists to help pay its debts.

Colonists dumped 90,000 pounds (40,823 kilograms) of tea into Boston Harbor during the Boston Tea Party.

Fight for Freedom

The colonists were angry about the new taxes. In 1770, Massachusetts colonists threw snowballs and stones at British soldiers. The soldiers opened fire, killing five people in what became known as the Boston Massacre. Then in 1773, colonists carried out the Boston Tea Party. They sneaked aboard three British ships in Boston Harbor and dumped the ships' cargo of tea into the water. After that, Great Britain passed even harsher laws. The colonists fought back, and the Revolutionary War (1775–1783) began.

Paul Revere

On April 18, 1775, British soldiers headed for Concord, Massachusetts. They were ordered to destroy colonial supplies of weapons. But Paul Revere set out on horseback to warn the colonial **militia** of the plan. Revere was a silversmith from Boston. He rode from Boston to Concord. Along the way, he alerted patriots that the British were coming. Gunshots were fired between colonists and British soldiers at Lexington, Massachusetts. The Revolutionary War had begun!

Growing State

Massachusetts did well after the war. Boston became a busy port city. Its ships carried goods around the world. **Textile** factories sprung up around Massachusetts. Many people working in these factories were **immigrants** from places such as Germany, Ireland, and Poland. They worked long hours in poor conditions for low pay. Children— some as young as seven—worked in factories, too.

Timeline of Massachusetts Events

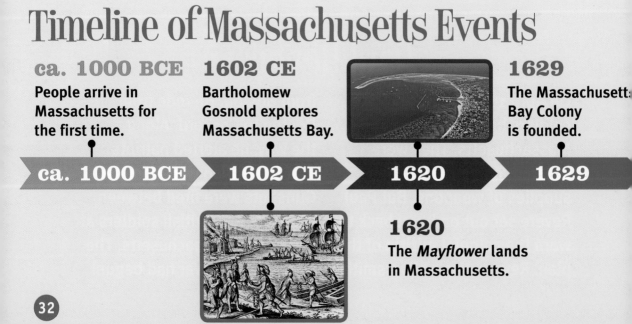

ca. 1000 BCE
People arrive in Massachusetts for the first time.

1602 CE
Bartholomew Gosnold explores Massachusetts Bay.

1629
The Massachusett Bay Colony is founded.

ca. 1000 BCE → 1602 CE → 1620 → 1629

1620
The *Mayflower* lands in Massachusetts.

Leading the Way

Massachusetts has worked to improve its people's lives. It was the first state to ban children under 15 from working. The state also founded the country's first public school and public library. Massachusetts helped lead the **abolitionists** in the 1800s. A century later, state leaders were fighting for **civil rights**. Then in 2006, Massachusetts became the first state to require that all its citizens have access to health care.

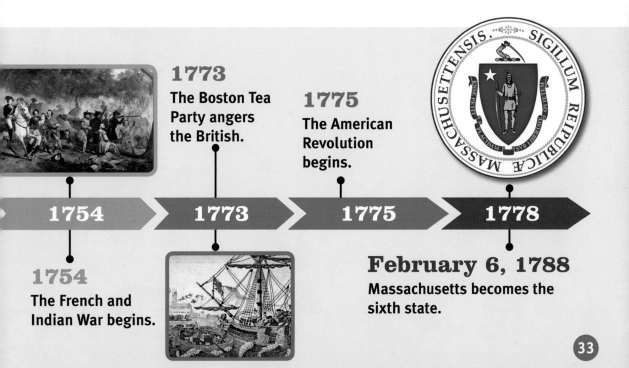

1773
The Boston Tea Party angers the British.

1775
The American Revolution begins.

1754 | **1773** | **1775** | **1778**

1754
The French and Indian War begins.

February 6, 1788
Massachusetts becomes the sixth state.

Street performers can often be seen in Boston.

A street performer does tricks for an audience during New Year's Eve festivities in Boston.

CHAPTER 4

Culture

Today, nearly seven million people call Massachusetts home. The state's original colonists were from England. But a wave of Irish immigrants arrived in the 1840s. Now they are the largest group in the state. Today, people from all over the world live in Massachusetts. The state's Native American cultures remain, as well. But only two of the seven original Algonquin groups that lived in the state still exist.

The Boston Marathon has been held every year since 1897.

Outstanding Sports

Massachusetts is big on sports. Die-hard baseball fans pack Fenway Park to see the Boston Red Sox. The New England Patriots are five-time Super Bowl champions. Hockey fans follow the Boston Bruins, while basketball fans cheer on the Boston Celtics.

One of Massachusetts's biggest annual sporting events is the Boston Marathon. About 30,000 people participate in this long-distance foot race each year!

State Celebrations

The people of Massachusetts enjoy participating in a variety of annual traditions. Each March, Boston hosts a big St. Patrick's Day parade. The state's huge Irish population turns out to show pride in their heritage. Other yearly events celebrate the state's many local food specialties, such as cranberries, scallops, and clam chowder.

People line the streets waiting for the annual St. Patrick's Day parade to go by.

Big Businesses

Many people in Massachusetts have jobs in education. The state has more than 120 colleges and universities! Hospitals employ many people, as well. Massachusetts also has more **biotechnology** companies than any other state. Many of the state's people continue to farm and fish for a living. Factories still produce goods such as scientific instruments, processed foods, and books. Thanks to Massachusetts's beaches and historic sites, tourism is thriving in the state.

Cambridge has become an important site for biotechnology companies in recent years.

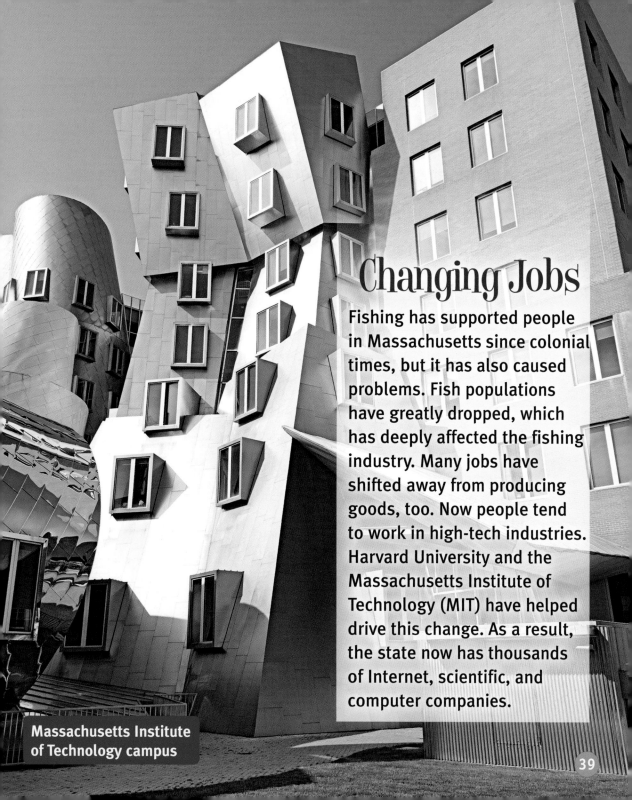

Changing Jobs

Fishing has supported people in Massachusetts since colonial times, but it has also caused problems. Fish populations have greatly dropped, which has deeply affected the fishing industry. Many jobs have shifted away from producing goods, too. Now people tend to work in high-tech industries. Harvard University and the Massachusetts Institute of Technology (MIT) have helped drive this change. As a result, the state now has thousands of Internet, scientific, and computer companies.

Massachusetts Institute of Technology campus

Food Traditions

History and local products shape the food in Massachusetts. Slow-cooked Boston baked beans are based on an Algonquin recipe. Clam chowder is a soup first made by colonists. Homegrown cranberries and Concord grapes are also on the menu. For dessert there is Boston cream pie, a cream-filled vanilla cake topped with chocolate.

★ Clam Chowder ★

Ask an adult to help you!

This seafood soup is a New England favorite. Top it with oyster crackers to add a crunchy texture.

Ingredients

2 (10-ounce) cans minced clams (drain the clams and keep the clam juice)

3 cups potatoes, peeled and cubed

1 onion, chopped

1 teaspoon salt

$\frac{1}{4}$ teaspoon pepper

3 cups milk

3 tablespoons flour

Directions

Combine clam juice, potatoes, onion, salt, and pepper in a large pot. Bring to a boil over high heat, and then lower the heat and simmer the soup for 15 minutes. Add the clams, milk, and flour. Cover the pot and cook for about 5 minutes longer. Serve and enjoy!

A tour guide talks with students along Boston's Freedom Trail. This trail is a 2.5-mile (4 km) path past 16 important locations in American history.

A Great State

Massachusetts is brimming with history. No wonder about 30 million people visit it each year! Both visitors and residents can explore America's roots. In Massachusetts, people can visit important sites of the American Revolution and even walk in the steps of the country's Founding Fathers and discover how these patriots helped make the country what it is today. The state's rich past is just one reason why Massachusetts is great! ★

Famous People

Benjamin Franklin

(1706–1790) was a statesman and scientist who developed the lightning rod, bifocal glasses, and the Franklin stove, among other inventions.

Phillis Wheatley

(1753?–1784) was a former slave who later became the first published African American poet.

Samuel Morse

(1791–1872) invented the electric telegraph and created the Morse code to use with his machine. He was also a painter.

Frederick Douglass

(1818?–1895) escaped slavery to become an abolitionist, writer, speaker, and statesman.

Susan B. Anthony

(1820–1906) was a women's rights activist who helped women win the right to vote.

Emily Dickinson

(1830–1886) was a poet who wrote more than 1,700 poems.

Alexander Graham Bell

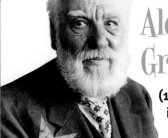

(1847–1922) was the inventor known for creating the telephone.

W. E. B. Du Bois

(1868–1963) was a civil rights activist and cofounder of the National Association for the Advancement of Colored People (NAACP).

Theodor Seuss Geisel

(1904–1991) wrote children's books, such as *The Cat in the Hat* and *The Lorax*, under the name Dr. Seuss.

John F. Kennedy

(1917–1963) was the 35th president of the United States. He was in office from 1961 until his assassination in 1963.

Did You Know That...

Four U.S. presidents were born in Massachusetts: John Adams, John Quincy Adams, John F. Kennedy, and George H. W. Bush.

Whitman resident Ruth Wakefield invented chocolate chip cookies in the 1930s. She first served them to guests at her hotel, the Toll House Inn.

Massachusetts farmers grow about two million barrels of cranberries each year.

Massachusetts has more than 300 museums.

The state is home to the country's oldest park, Boston Common, which was established in 1634.

Massachusetts fishers catch about 260 million pounds (118 million kg) of seafood each year.

Did you find the truth?

(F) Massachusetts is named after the ship its first settlers arrived on.

(T) Cranberries are one of Massachusetts's biggest crops.

Resources

Books

Nonfiction

Cunningham, Kevin. *The Massachusetts Colony*. New York: Scholastic, 2011.

Krull, Kathleen. *What Was the Boston Tea Party?* New York: Grosset & Dunlap, 2013.

Prince, April Jones. *Who Was Frederick Douglass?* New York: Grosset & Dunlap, 2014.

Fiction

Alcott, Louisa May. *Little Women*. Boston: Roberts Brothers, 1868.

Chari, Sheela. *Vanished*. New York: Disney/Hyperion Books, 2011.

Forbes, Esther. *Johnny Tremain, a Novel for Old & Young*. Boston: Houghton Mifflin Company, 1943.

Movies

Hocus Pocus (1993)

Jaws (1975)

National Treasure (2004)

The Perfect Storm (2000)

That Darn Cat (1997)

Visit this Scholastic website for more information on Massachusetts:

★ www.factsfornow.scholastic.com
Enter the keyword **Massachusetts**

Important Words

abolitionists (ab-uh-LISH-uh-nists) people who supported the end of slavery in the United States

allies (AL-eyez) people, groups, or nations working together

biotechnology (bye-oh-tek-NAH-luh-jee) altering living organisms to develop medicines, improve food production, or dispose of wastes

bogs (BAHGZ) areas of wet, marshy ground where the soil is made up mostly of rotting plant material

civil rights (SIV-uhl RITEZ) rights that give people full legal, social, and economic equality

endangered (en-DAYN-jurd) in danger of becoming extinct, usually because of human activity

immigrants (IM-uh-gruhntz) people who move to another country

militia (muh-LISH-uh) an army of citizens trained to serve as soldiers

peninsula (puh-NIN-suh-luh) a piece of land sticking out into a body of water

persecution (pur-suh-KYOO-shuhn) being harassed or oppressed because of someone's beliefs, ethnicity, race, gender, or identity

textile (TEK-stile) cloth material used for making clothing and other products

Index

Page numbers in **bold** indicate illustrations.

About the Author

Cody Crane is an award-winning children's writer. She specializes in nonfiction and has written about everything from hibernating bears to roller coasters. Before becoming an author, she was set on becoming a scientist. But she discovered that sharing science, art, history, and other interesting topics with a young audience was even better. Crane lives in Houston, Texas, with her husband and son.